Old SHETTLESTON and TOLLCROSS

by
Rhona Wilson

D0921894

Rockdove Gardens are opposite what was once the site of the Deer Park; Maukinfauld Road turns off on the right. Legend has it that during the block's construction the builder visited Ireland, winning so much money on a horse called Rockdove that he named the buildings after it.

© Stenlake Publishing 1998
First published in the United Kingdom, 1998,
by Stenlake Publishing, Ochiltree Sawmill, The Lade,
Ochiltree, Ayrshire, KA18 2NX
Telephone / Fax: 01290 423114

ISBN 1 84033 053 8

Tollcross Central Church, erected 1806, was demolished after it was gutted by fire in 1990, although its gates and halls (to the right) are still standing. In Tollcross argument rages over whether Willie Miller (author of 'Wee Willie Winkie') is buried in Tollcross Cemetery or at the grander Eastern Necropolis, which was once part of Tollcross lands. A wood-turner by trade, Miller spent his free time writing children's songs and poems, eventually getting a collection published in 1863. He died just nine years later, with funds raised by locals used to erect a memorial to him at the Necropolis. Apparently the money was raised while Miller was alive to support him after he became ill in 1871. His body does in fact lie in Tollcross Cemetery although those searching for proof will experience difficulties since his grave is unmarked.

INTRODUCTION

Shettleston and Tollcross are centuries old; both districts formed part of the lands of 'Schedinistun', gifted to the Bishop of Glasgow by Alexander II in 1242. No one can be certain what Shettleston's name derives from, although references to a *villam filie sedin* in the twelfth century suggest that the village was then known as 'the residence of Sedin's daughter', perhaps in honour of some ancient settler. An explanation put forward in the nineteenth century, that the name developed from a corruption of 'Shuttleston' (on account of it being a weaving village) is less credible. The origins of the name Tollcross are more straightforward: it derives from the Scots' word *towl*, one of the meanings of which is 'toll' or 'to count', and it is thought that Rutherglen Burgh had the right to charge tolls on goods entering and leaving the district at Tollcross.

For centuries both villages were essentially a collection of hamlets, Shettleston being made up of Shettleston, Westmuir, Sandyhills and Middle Quarter, and Tollcross being grouped with Fullarton and Auchenshuggle. Shettleston was the larger of the two settlements, considered to be 'of a fair size' by the 1500s when its agricultural community made a living producing oats, barley and pease. By the late 1700s Tollcross's main street was lined with weavers' and tradesmen's cottages, the first of which were built at what is now Amulree Street. Shettleston was populated by weavers as well as agricultural workers by the early nineteenth century.

Although known to be present in the district, coal didn't become a significant factor in the local economy until the eighteenth and nineteenth centuries. A John Gray was listed in records of 1564 as a collier, but it is likely that he would have worked primitive drift mines. These shallow-sloping mines tended to be plagued with cave-ins and prone to flooding; when these problems became overwhelming a mine would be abandoned and a new one started elsewhere. The Industrial Revolution brought new technologies, such as the Newcomen steam engine, which made mining at deeper levels possible by allowing water to be pumped out of workings. The Gray, McNair and Dunlop families can be credited with introducing large-scale industry to Shettleston and Tollcross, the former two through their mining interests and the latter by developing the Clyde Ironworks, which they took over in the early 1800s.

The latter half of the nineteenth century saw rapid expansion in both villages, with the distinctions between their composite hamlets becoming less clearly defined as development progressed. Eastbank Academy, built in 1894 and known by the villagers as 'Scott's Folly' on account of its grandeur, seems to have been symbolic of a village changing too quickly for its inhabitants' liking.

The railway line opened by the North British Railway in 1871 provided the impetus to exploit Shettleston and Tollcross's coalfields on a larger scale, allowing mined coal to be transported to Glasgow and elsewhere. At the same time local demand for coal soared too, with concerns such as the Shettleston Ironworks and Beardmore's Forge at Parkhead requiring huge quantities. Shettleston's population doubled between 1890 and 1900, but even at this early stage there were suggestions that the lucrative mines were being worked out; a newspaper article of 1894 claimed that in Shettleston, miners were 'a diminished and diminishing quantity'.

The mines of both villages were largely exhausted by the 1930s. Over the following decades the iron and steel industries went into decline, and Parkhead's famous forge is now the site of a shopping and leisure complex. In recent years the most significant development has been the formation of housing associations, such as Shettleston's in 1977, set up to encourage stability in the population by providing good quality affordable housing. Despite this, Shettleston in particular is still categorised as an area with a high turnover of population. Tollcross was once considered 'the aristocratic and exclusive part of Shettleston' (a label which incensed Tollcrossians, who were unwilling to be associated with Shettleston under any circumstances), but it is unlikely that anyone would describe it as posh today. Despite being run-down, however, Shettleston and Tollcross have both survived; neither have become the 'ghost towns' that was the fate of many other mining villages. Shettleston's main street and shops are permanently teeming with people, while its rail link provides a ten minute journey into Glasgow for commuters. Tollcross still benefits from its location around Tollcross Park, and that centrepiece has recently benefited from the building of a large leisure centre and the allocation of lottery funds to renovate its old glasshouses.

SANDYHILLS HOUSE. SHETTLESTON
BRANDON SERIES

Sandyhills House. Documents of the seventeenth century mention 'Sandihillis' although the mansion house pictured here wasn't built until the mid-1800s. The Sandyhills Estate was originally owned by the Corbett family who sold it to two Glasgow merchants, William Broch and John Miller in 1756, at a time when many merchants and tobacco lords were buying country seats. Just two years later Sandyhills became the lands of the Galloway family. In 1781 John Galloway rented farmland on the estate to John McMillan (minister of the Reformed Presbyterian Church) who lived and worked there to supplement his stipend. The church's first meeting house was built on the estate, and its twelve hour summer services proved so popular that the congregation spilled out into the surrounding fields which became known as 'the preaching braes'. It is thought that the old thatched church was demolished together with the farmhouse when the mansion house was built.

YORK TERRACE AND SANDYHILLS, SHETTLESTON.

In 1794 the hamlet of Sandyhills had a population of 341 and even in 1924 it was considered small enough for its new housing scheme to seem out of place. The *Glasgow Eastern Standard* proclaimed that the scheme had 'grown in a night', going on to compare its speedy evolution to the rise of prairie towns. Not all were impressed, Bailie Dollan in particular criticising the design of the new homes. The scheme was a turning point for the appearance of the district, which had previously included the fields that separated Shettleston and Tollcross. Sandyhills Farm and House became the site of Meadowlea and Hawthorn Lea housing schemes. The new St Paul's Chapel stands on the site of the white cottage in this picture. The first chapel (built in 1857) was run by Father Patrick McLaughlin. He was imprisoned for fifteen days because he refused to name a thief who returned money during confession, and became something of a local hero as a result.

This tram was photographed travelling along Baillieston Road from Shettleston to Garrowhill in August 1960. Sandyhills Church is in the background on the left. John Thomson, minister of Shettleston Parish Church, established Sandyhills Church when he seceded following the Disruption of 1843. A 'Ten Years Conflict' had raged in the Church of Scotland over whether or not the state could interfere in its internal affairs. In 1842 Scottish ministers threatened a secession if the Government didn't affirm the church's right to self-rule. That same year Thomson lost his wife and three children to illness over a three month period, but despite his personal tragedy felt impelled to join the 400 ministers who walked out in 1843 to form the Free Church. The first Sandyhills Church was built in 1854 and was replaced by a larger building *circa* 1899. This eventually became unsafe due to mine workings and has since been demolished and replaced.

Budhill Avenue, with Budhill Square to the left. This area got its name from Budhill Farm which was once situated in the factory district between Annick Street and Shettleston Station. Many of the tenements date from the late nineteenth century and were built as a direct result of the railway opening. Shettleston's building boom between 1860 and 1905 reflected the district's industrial boom, but unfortunately left a legacy of appalling Victorian inner-city conditions. John Wheatley's Housing Act of 1924 went some way towards addressing the problems but even by the 1970s some Shettleston residents were living in dreadful circumstances, with their homes still lit by gas in some cases. In general there were three 'room and kitchen' properties and a 'single-end' on each tenement landing. Hot water was rare and sometimes up to six households had to share an outside toilet.

Shettleston Station.

Public transport in Shettleston in the early nineteenth century consisted of horse coaches; in 1837 six left for Edinburgh each day on a journey that could take over four hours. The North British Railway's line from Shettleston to Edinburgh (opened in 1871) changed all that, although its primary purpose was to serve the village's burgeoning coal and iron industries. An extension to Hamilton opened for passenger traffic on 1 April 1878 and doubled the number of trains passing through Shettleston. In 1894 the station-master, David Lawson, stated in an interview with the *Glasgow Weekly Herald* that Shettleston Station processed around 500 season tickets a year and that goods traffic had recently risen from 400 to 4,000 tons a month.

SHETTLESTON N.B. RAILWAY STATION. 625

An annual published in 1911 recorded that 'Shettleston received a large amount of attention some years ago on account of subsidences which threatened to entomb the North British Railway Station'. Prickliesmuir Pit was to its north, and despite the danger of subsidence the station has survived and is still open. Shettleston became part of Glasgow in 1912 and for many years the Sandyhills railway bridge marked the boundary between Glasgow and Lanarkshire; as you walked over the bridge you went from one county to the other. The Grange, a house at the southern end of Sandyhills Bridge, was known as the last house in Shettleston. Today, Shettleston's station buildings and bridge have been replaced, although the tenements in the centre, part of Budhill Square, are still standing. The lands in the middle of the square have been landscaped.

983/12.

EASTMUIR, SHETTLESTON.

Although this postcard is captioned Eastmuir Street, this stretch of road is now classed as Shettleston Road, with present day Eastmuir Street featuring as part of the Annick Street Industrial Estate. The site of old Shettleston Kirk is further down the road on the left. Its graveyard is intact despite the demolition of the building, which was described by one commentator in 1905 as being 'far from a thing of beauty'. Originally built as a 'preaching station' because of the four mile walk to Barony Church in Glasgow, it was disjoined from its mother church in 1847. In 1903 it was replaced by a new building in Killin Street, paid for by subscription; Rev. John White (known for visiting parishioners on his horse Victor) had to take landmark legal action to force absentee landowners to pay their share. The gates of the old graveyard are flanked by sentry boxes which were used for all-night vigils during the times of the body-snatchers. Some of the gravestones date back as far as 1765 although most of the inscriptions are now illegible.

Eastbank Academy, Shettleston.

Eastbank Academy, built in the early 1890s to replace Eastmuir School, was referred to derisively as 'Scott's Folly' when it first opened. Dr Alexander Scott, chairman of the school board, pushed through the project on account of Shettleston's rising population, although locals thought it was far too grand for a village. In the end Scott's instinct proved correct with 1,127 pupils on the roll by 1901. The school acquired a formidable reputation, and just ten years later a new primary department was built in Academy Street, with the thirties seeing the old Eastmuir building in use once again as a temporary measure to satisfy increasing demand for places. A new school, proposed in 1938, was scuppered by the onset of the Second World War and after a long campaign by the local MP, councillors and churches, was finally built in 1986. The academy was renamed the John Wheatley College after a refurbishment programme.

MAIN STREET SHETTLESTON FROM ROSSLYN PLACE. 650.

Shettleston Road looking east towards Eastbank Academy. Born in County Waterford in 1869, John Wheatley moved to Bargeddie with his family when he was aged nine. Thirteen of them shared a single end with no water supply or sanitation facilities. Two years later Wheatley started work down the mines, eventually setting up a grocer's business with his brother in 1893. This was unsuccessful but a later publishing venture took off. His Catholic Socialist Society (est. 1906) made him unpopular with those who believed that politics and religion shouldn't be mixed. When he was elected to Glasgow City Council he began campaigning for subsidised housing with a pamphlet entitled *£8 Cottages for Glasgow Citizens*; his slogan was 'homes not hutches'. The Independent Labour Party, which he joined in 1908, finally gave him the opportunity to put his ideas into practice. He was MP for Shettleston in 1922 and Minister of Health in the 1924 Government; although he was in office for only nine months he successfully proposed the Wheatley Act which made subsidies available to local authorities, enabling them to build decent housing and offer reduced rents. Wheatley's views became increasing left-wing which didn't endear him to the next Government. He wasn't offered office in 1929 and died the following year.

Shettleston Road looking east. The mid-twentieth century solution to Shettleston's housing problem was demolition. In the 1950s and 60s the local authority pulled down hundreds of tenements (450 buildings were demolished in Shettleston alone in the early seventies) and relocated their residents in the 'brave new world' housing schemes such as Easterhouse and Drumchapel. Unfortunately this created another set of problems; built with a lack of infrastructure and facilities, these alternative towns propagated the poverty, unemployment and poor living conditions they had been built to address. It took much campaigning from local groups to change the emphasis to renovation with the 1974 Housing Act, which introduced the Housing Association Grant, helping matters greatly. Shettleston Housing Association was formed two years later and is still building today.

Looking west along Shettleston Road with Chester Street to the right. John Wheatley's successor as MP for Shettleston in 1930 was John McGovern. Born in Coatbridge in 1887, he left for Australia in the early 1920s, later returning to Shettleston to work as a plumber. McGovern was the leader of the Hunger Marches from Glasgow to London during the Depression of the thirties. In 1933 he protested in the House of Lords about cuts to unemployment benefit and the means-testing of benefits. He joined the Labour Party in 1947, becoming involved in the moral re-armament movement of the cold war years. McGovern became increasingly right wing in the years before his death in 1968.

Thatched Houses & The Drum Shettleston Brandon Series

The Drum Pub, the small building on the left between the cottages and the tenement, was owned by John Reid who worked as a miner while his wife ran the bar. Dog Pit, which got its name because someone dropped an unwanted dog into it and started a trend, was behind The Drum. Shettleston's Kirk House bar, established near the old church in 1770, claims to be one of the oldest pubs in Glasgow. A chronicler of 1860 detailed some of the entertainments held there such as 'blin' bookings', a custom in which two young people were chosen to 'get married' and thereafter stood the evening's expenses. Upstairs there was dancing to Fiddler Stinson, with men paying a penny a reel for the music. The Drum and the small row of thatched cottages next to it (known as Dickson's Row and still extant in 1906), later became the site of Shettleston Co-op.

No.2

Main Street, Shettleston

Shettleston Co-op was founded in 1882 and was successful enough to be able to build tenements in Shettleston Road and South Vesalius Street fifteen years later. These had shops on the ground floor with flats above. The Co-op carried out more building in Pettigrew Street, erecting offices, a creamery and halls between 1910 and 1912. By 1915 it ran fifteen shops in the village and just after the end of World War I amalgamated with the Chryston Co-op. It traded profitably throughout the next few decades but began to flounder in the sixties due to increased competition from supermarkets and the general depression of the area. In 1980 it joined forces with Coatbridge Co-op to form the East Strathclyde Co-operative Society which survived just two years. This was eventually sold to CWS Ltd.

By the 1960s and 70s many nineteenth century tenements were in a fragile state, and several Shettleston properties were served Dangerous Building notices. A demolition job at 1002 Shettleston Road (above) in the late 70s resulted in tragedy. Barber Joe Eusebi and his customer John Wilson both died when two floors of the tenement collapsed into the hairdressing shop below; Eusebi's eighteen year old son escaped because he was out on an errand. Despite the fact that the adjoining building had fallen apart three months previously, inspectors had found 'no cause for concern' when they viewed the building which Mr Eusebi's shop occupied two days beforehand. It took four hours to recover the bodies with Glasgow's ambulance drivers breaking their 24 hour strike to help. The building had originally been four floors high and was having its upper storeys demolished at the instigation of Mr Eusebi, in order to save his ground level shop. Politicians later protested at the widespread practice of shops continuing to trade while demolition work was being carried out above them.

Shettleston Cross. Coal had been mined in Shettleston on a small scale for centuries prior to the Industrial Revolution. The early operations were unsophisticated, with workers sinking bell-pits (vertical shafts opened out at the bottom) or simply mining coal from an outcrop and following the seam underground via gently sloping drift mines (whose openings were known as 'ingoing eyes'). By the beginning of the eighteenth century the increasing demand for coal meant that some of the technical problems, such as flooding, had to be solved to allow colliers to mine at deeper levels. Newcomen's steam engine, later improved by James Watt, was the first real innovation. The Gray family of Carntyne and the McNairs of Greenfield became the main coalmasters of the district, their Westmuir pits supplying Glasgow with large quantities of coal. The first Newcomen engine in Glasgow was installed by the Grays at a Carntyne pit in 1768. Up to that point alternative methods of drainage included John Gray's windmill pump, which was in use for three years from 1737 until it was destroyed in a storm.

Taken around 1909, this shot shows clear differences from the previous photograph with a new tenement block on the left-hand corner across the road from what is now the Cottage Bar. Improvements in mining technology meant that the new large-scale industries could be supplied with the huge quantities of coal that they required. Coal was vital to the iron industry, for instance, and with works such as Beardmore's Forge just down the road, the coalmasters of the east end of Glasgow had a ready market for their product. Shettleston-born James Neilson's hot blast process for smelting iron ore was developed in the late 1820s at the nearby Clyde Ironworks.

Despite improvements in technology, high water levels continued to be a problem at many Shettleston pits. The situation was made worse because, although several colliery owners were affected, their competitiveness prevented them from tackling the problem together. Caroline Pit (in the vicinity of present day Caroline Street) was often flooded by water from adjacent collieries, but this was of little concern to anyone except her owner. Auld Prickie Pit at the McNairs' Greenfield Colliery had to be abandoned for use as a basin for overflows elsewhere, and it was actually the Gray family which installed a pump in it to prevent flooding in their Westmuir colliery. Over time the Grays realised they couldn't cope single-handedly and asked for financial help from owners of nearby collieries such as Sandyhills and Peesweep. They all refused with the result that the Westmuir colliery was abandoned in 1875 and all the collieries which had relied on its drainage systems were flooded. It is said that today the water still lies under Shettleston as a vast, underground lake.

THE CROSS, SHETTLESTON.

BRANDON SERIES.

There were a lot of working pits in Shettleston as late as 1910, although a newspaper article of about fifteen years earlier stated that factories had overtaken both agriculture and mining as the main means of making a living. By the end of the First World War many Shettleston pits were spent. Over the next decade most of the remainder closed down, and most traces of the industry had gone by the thirties. Part of the Greenfield Estate became a golf course in the early 1900s, the remainder of it being developed as Greenfield Park and a housing scheme in later years. New houses have been built along the stretch of Shettleston Road on the left where the trees are standing.

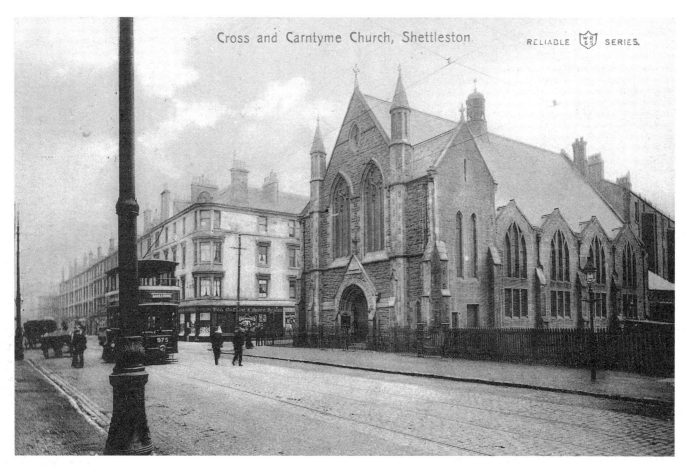

A free church was established in Shettleston c.1884 with James Allan as minister; Carntyne Church, at Shettleston Cross, was built in 1893 to house the congregation. It now has links with Eastbank Church. Between the mid-1880s and 90s Shettleston's population doubled to reach 14,000. Many clubs were set up during this period, including the Shettleston Cricket Club (1893) and the Springboig Tennis Club (1895). The Tabernacle Gospel Hall, located at 242 Old Shettleston Road, had a large congregation, and held children's meetings as well as church services. These were attended by as many as 600 children who watched lantern slide shows organised by David Reid and listened to speakers including one Mr Muir, a herbalist with a large business on Great Western Road. The Gospel Hall's Sunday School was also very well attended and held a popular annual outing. During the 1940s Alex Holden, a member of the church, used his open lorry to transport the crowds to their destination. Long wooden seats from the church were placed on the back of the lorry and roped together, and Mr Holden shuttled back and forth until everyone had reached Millerston park, or wherever the outing was to be held.

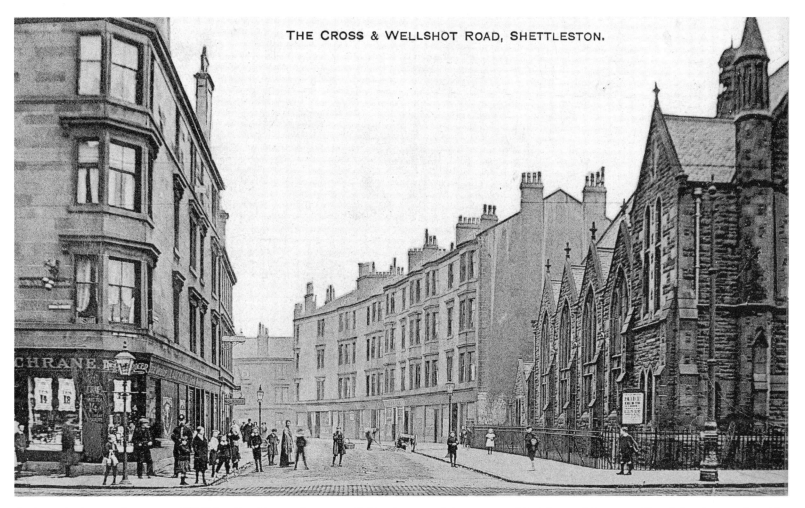

Cochrane's shop on the corner of Wellshot Road is now known as Calder Stores and the tenement block beyond Carntyne Church has been replaced by new housing. Shettleston had various industries in addition to mining and ironmaking. A rope works was established there around 1877 and was still standing (although disused) a century later; the narrow buildings which make up a rope-walk don't lend themselves very readily to adaptation. Other businesses included a brickworks (just outwith the Shettleston boundary) and the Carntyne Dyewood Mills built at 576 Shettleston Road in the early 1880s for McArthur, Scott and Co.

Modern flats now fill the gap between the two tenements at the top right hand corner of this picture of Wellshot Road. A prominent Shettleston factory of the twentieth century was the North British Bottleworks which opened *c.*1904 on the site of Shettleston House. At the time there were about fifty bottle works in Glasgow supplying the liquor trade with bottles for wine, beer and spirits. The works closed in 1983 with the last bottle off the production line taken as an exhibit by the Peoples' Palace.

This photograph and the following two were taken at James and John Murdoch's Carntyne Farm; the latter brother was well-known as a competition judge and breeder of Ayrshire cattle. Although primitive mining took place in Shettleston district as early as the sixteenth century it was principally an agricultural area until the nineteenth century, with its lands particularly suited to growing oats, barley and pease. Other farms in the area included Shettleston Farm (at Edrom Street) and Middle Quarter Farm (at what is now the corner of Fenella Street and Shettleston Road). Despite the village's industrial development, cattle were still being herded along its main street in 1910 and there were at least two working farms in the district in the 1960s. The 'homes for heroes' scheme of the inter-war years played as big a part as industry in changing the area's rural appearance. Southern Shettleston became the Sandyhills Housing Scheme with the Carntyne farmlands also making way for housing.

Carntyne Farm. The Gray family owned Carntyne Estate for over 200 years and Robert Gray had Carntyne House built in 1802. The family was known for its radical streak – legend has it that one of its female members, 'an old aunt', stole a mason's mallet during the building of St Andrews-on-the-Green Episcopal Church. This was the first church to be built after the Reformation with an organ and it is said that the disapproving aunt hid the tool in her muff in an attempt to halt building work, berating it as a 'house of Baal [false god or idol]'. The family line ended in the 1867 when the last member died without issue and was buried in the family lair at Glasgow Cathedral.

Carntyne Farm. Before the Industrial Revolution there was an agricultural revolution, during which farming methods were improved leading to greater yields. Innovations included drainage tiles, which allowed waterlogged land to be reclaimed for agriculture and were among the products made by Shettleston man John Anderson in the mid-nineteenth century. Enclosure of land with hedging or fencing provided shelter and meant that crops could be managed more easily and protected from damage by animals. Law, Duncan and Co., tool-makers in Shettleston, managed to bridge the gap between agriculture and industry. In the 1850s Robert Law was producing wooden agricultural tools along with new equipment such as iron ploughs and threshing machines. The company subsequently advertised that it built railway waggons and iron houses. Its works were replaced by J. and T. Boyd's Shettleston Ironworks around 1875. By 1894 the company employed 500 people and produced machinery for the textile industry until at least 1974.

It is thought that Larchgrove House was built some time around 1700 and modernised by later owners including the Adam family who bought it in 1853. John Adam JP owned the estate in 1910. In the past its grounds were a popular venue for summer events such as cattle shows and Sunday School trips. Larchgrove House was eventually demolished and its grounds used to accommodate the Larchgrove Remand Home for young people.

Shettleston and Tollcross's rising population in the 1890s resulted in an increase in the number of schools in the district. In 1864 Shettleston, for example, had only one school with 100 pupils, whereas thirty years later there were six serving over 2,000 pupils. Wellshot Public School, opposite the leisure centre, was built in 1904 as a junior secondary and was later used as a primary school. Earlier schools in Tollcross included one at the ironworks *c.*1786 and a church school dating from 1826.

Wellshot Road, Tollcross.

It is difficult to place the site of Green's Cinema, known locally as 'the fleapit' or 'the scum'. All the tenements to its right have been demolished, as was the cinema itself in the 1960s after a stint as a bingo hall. The building was replaced by the small, flat-roofed Cock Robin Pub (named after the famous exhibit at Tollcross Museum) which later became the Carrington but is now closed. This area of Tollcross is known as 'Egypt', and is marked as such on old Glasgow tram maps which gave names to fare stages. The derivation stems from Egypt Farm, which was supposedly established by a soldier on his return from service in that country. Owned by the Hamilton family until 1983, Egypt Farm was just off Dalness Street and was mainly a dairy concern.

Tollcross Park Lodge. Alexander II granted the Tollcross lands, stretching from the Eastern Necropolis to Sandyhills, to the powerful Corbet family in 1242. The Corbets retained ownership of the entire estate for over five centuries until 1756 when they sold Sandyhills. Some years later the remainder of the estate passed into the hands of the Dunlops of Carmyle, known for their varied business interests. When the family's tobacco firm failed in 1793 it was able to fall back on its mining interests at Fullarton, getting a good return on the £10,000 they invested in the colliery over the 1777-1793 period.

Tollcross House replaced an earlier house and was built by David Bryce for the Dunlop family in 1848. Just over fifty years later it was sold, together with its grounds, to Glasgow Corporation, for development into a public park and children's museum. The museum opened in 1905 with its Cock Robin display – a selection of stuffed birds arranged in a glass case describing the poem *Who Killed Cock Robin?* – becoming a favourite exhibit. Due to financial strictures the museum finally closed in the seventies and lay empty for some time while politicians decided what to do with it. A suggestion that the old mansion should be developed into luxury flats was much opposed by locals and the building was reopened as a sheltered housing complex in 1993. 'Cock Robin' lay in a storeroom in Kelvingrove Museum until it was renovated as part of the Glasgow City of Culture celebrations of 1990.

Tollcross Park Gate, on Tollcross Road, is still standing. The Clyde Ironworks were established by Thomas Edington and William Cadell in 1786 to exploit local coal and ironstone, and eventually came into the ownership of the Dunlops of Tollcross. By the early 1790s 300 were employed at the works, which produced simple cast iron goods such as pots and pans. Later developments meant that pig iron could be converted into bar iron at a cheap enough price to undercut imports. In 1816 Colin Dunlop took over the business and encouraged experimentation which benefitted the whole iron industry. It was at the Clyde Works in 1828 that J.B. Neilson perfected his 'hot blast' process, which reduced the cost of iron production dramatically.

The bandstand, Tollcross Park. Conditions at the Clyde Ironworks were shocking by today's standards. Employees worked twelve hour shifts (beginning at six in the morning) and generally lived nearby in company houses such as the rows of single-room dwellings near Causewayside Street. Their wages were paid monthly and a truck shop system was in operation. Wages could be paid early as long as roughly 70% of them were spent in company-run shops, such as the Clyde Store in Causewayside Street. Goods in the truck shops were renowned for being overpriced and of poor quality, and a housewife resorting to the system one month might find herself locked forever in a vicious circle of not having enough cash to survive till the next pay day. The Clyde Store in particular had a reputation for short-changing its customers.

Tollcross Park. Accidents at the ironworks were sometimes fatal. In March 1939 Charles Phillips was crushed by a 20-foot wall which collapsed as a result of vibrations from a cement mixer. He was lucky enough to escape with just the loss of a leg, but three men casting a concrete floor a few weeks later were less fortunate. The platform they were standing on collapsed, burying them in a pile of debris which it took rescue workers an hour to fight their way through. Once the bodies were removed they had to be carried 500 yards through to the new works where the ambulance waggons were waiting. Ted Bone was the only one still alive when rescued from the scene of the accident; he later died at the Glasgow Royal Infirmary. In 1930 the Clyde Ironworks became part of the Colville group and remained in operation until the 1970s.

The bowling green, Tollcross Park. Bowling's history goes back to the Stone Age when it is thought that a primitive form of the game was played with rocks, using bones for markers. By the sixteenth century it was widespread throughout Europe and particularly popular in Scotland, where the earliest green was reputedly laid out at Holyrood Palace for James IV. Despite this royal patronage, the game quickly developed a bad reputation. Strange as it may seem, bowling was associated with drinking, gambling and general disorder and it remained a distinctly unrespectable pastime until its revival in the early nineteenth century. Again Scotland figured in the game's development, with the first set of rules being drawn up there in 1849.

Deer Park Gardens, overlooking Tollcross Park. The deer in the park were supposedly imported from Japan. Mini zoos were created at several of Glasgow's parks as people living in the inner city seldom or never got a chance to go to the countryside and see wildlife in its natural habitat. Elder Park in Govan also had deer and a llama at the turn of the century. Although the deer park at Tollcross has closed there is still an animal park, with inhabitants including goats and geese. A rose garden has been created on the site of the deer park, and the last deer to roam in the park, 'Bobby', has been stuffed and put on display in Tollcross Museum. The greenhouses in Tollcross Park formerly held a fine collection of orchids, on a par with Glasgow's other main collection in the Botanic Gardens. The old Shettleston swimming baths and tennis courts were also located within the park.

BRANDON SERIES.

DRUMOTHER MANSIONS, TOLLCROSS, GLASGOW.

Drumover Mansions. The word 'tenement' is derived from the Latin *tenementum*, meaning 'a holding'. From a plot of ground it came to mean a house (of whatever kind), but by the nineteenth century was being used exclusively with reference to domestic buildings of more than one storey with a communal entrance. The tenements of Drumover Mansions, in the 'posh' area of Tollcross, were better built and maintained than some of their ilk. Glasgow tenements were known for their overcrowding and squalor and one notorious close in the Drygate area accommodated 500 inhabitants. In the winter months local people brought their children to Drumover Brae to sledge down the hill to Tollcross Road.

Maukinfauld and Drumover Mansions with Ogilvie Street turning off on the right and Drumover Drive to the left. In 1973 the *Eastend News* printed its concerns about speeding on Tollcross Road, particularly the accident black-spot at the junction with Maukinfauld Road. This had long been a problem area with drivers racing round the corner regardless of the danger; just before the article was written a large lorry jack-knifed on the bend. The local authority's long-term plan was to straighten that part of the road by building on a section of the park.

Victoria Church started life as a Free Church congregation, formed some time after the Disruption of 1843. Previously its members had no meeting place and, despite falling numbers, a church was built at the instigation of Rev. James Drysdale in 1867. The Free Church became the Victoria Church in 1900 when it joined forces with Tollcross Central as part of the union of the Free and UP churches. A new building was deemed necessary around the same time and building began in 1901 at Main Street and Causewayside Street, adjacent to the old building which later became the church halls. The tenement block on the left has been demolished and was replaced by the low level Tollcross Youth Centre about eight years ago. Work actually started on the project about two years earlier but the original builder went bust leaving only a metal frame in place until the project was taken up by another firm.

Before London Road was created Tollcross Road was the main route out of Glasgow to the south. In fact most of the references to it in the Middle Ages are concerned with the repairs that were necessary to maintain this important route into Glasgow. About two thirds of the way down Causewayside Street is a pub which was originally a coaching inn with stables. The street name was changed from Main Street to Tollcross Road to avoid duplication when Tollcross became part of Glasgow in 1912.

Tollcross Road. The tramcars which transported passengers to Tollcross and Shettleston respectively, were the number 29 which went through Parkhead Cross, and the number 15, which after visiting Parkhead travelled down Westmuir Street, through Shettleston and on to Baillieston.

The two-storey building on the right hand side of Tollcross Road has been demolished, and further down the road there are some new flats close to Victoria Church. Most of the buildings to the left are intact, including the three-storey tenement with the Tudor style roof which serves as a useful local landmark. Macfarlane and Lang's biscuit factory, in Clydeford Drive, was established *c.*1925. In 1966 it became part of United Biscuits and is now known as the McVitie's factory. It currently employs about 1,000 people.

The large tenement to the right seems to have replaced the two-storey block in the right foreground of the previous picture. It is difficult to tell whether the small cottage beside it is still standing. The building on the spot today has similar dimensions, although it has been pebble-dashed and roofed with corrugated iron. The white cottage on the left in this picture has been demolished and is now the site of a billboard with waste ground behind it.

Tollcross's first Methodist Church in Altyre Street. Methodism (a Protestant sect known for its strict discipline) was first introduced to the village by George Joap who held meetings in his own home during the mid-nineteenth century. The congregation was large enough to join the 1st Glasgow Circuit in 1867 and the church pictured here was built five years later. The Tollcross section was very active in the East End and was credited with spreading the word to nearby villages such as Parkhead and Shettleston. The building was destroyed during a bad storm c.1911 and a replacement, which survived until the mid-seventies, was built on the site. Attendance began to fall from the 1950s onwards as local authorities decanted people from city tenements to new-build schemes such as Easterhouse and Drumchapel. The last sermon was read by Rev. Haddow Tennent in July 1976 and the building was left to an uncertain fate. It became a Masonic Lodge and was later used as an indoor market. The dilapidated church was demolished in 1991.

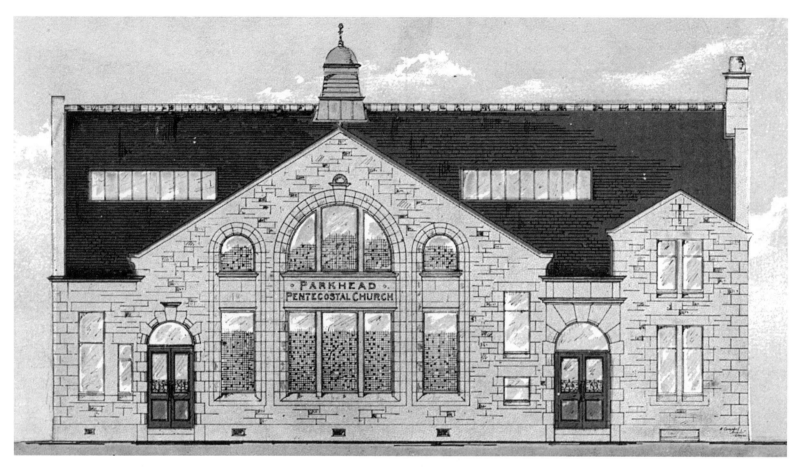

Known locally as the Sharpe Church, the Parkhead Pentecostal was opened in 1907. Its eighty-strong congregation helped raised funds for construction of the church using promotional postcards such as this one. The back of it reads: 'Dear _____ Rev. and Mrs. George Sharpe are here from Scotland in the interests of the "First Holiness Church in Scotland" and a Holiness Bible School. They are doing a splendid work. I am sure you would like to invest 25 cents or more in their cause. Kindly send to him, care Rev. Mr. Kunz, Mooers, N.Y. I am sending 12 Post Cards, which I hope will bring in at least three dollars. Please do not fail them, or Your Friend, _____.' The church, renamed the Sharpe Memorial Church of the Nazarene, is still standing, just off Burgher Street.

This tram has just turned off Shettleston Road into Westmuir Street on its way to Parkhead Cross. The tenement on the right is on the corner of Muiryfauld Street. The name 'Shettleston' may have derived from the Anglo-Saxon *sceaddan* (the sheddens), meaning a parting of ways. Documents of 1226 mention the 'Cross of Schedustun' and the power of Rutherglen royal burgh (which once had trading rights over Glasgow) to collect tolls in Glasgow but not at Shettleston Cross. Scholars have failed to reach agreement on where it may have been located at that time. Present-day Shettleston Cross was considered an unlikely site for the sheddens, which was thought to have been nearer to town, perhaps at Parkhead Cross where an ancient ford of the Clyde may have provided access from Rutherglen. The siting of the cross outwith Shettleston village, however, seems to quash any attempts to suggest that 'Shettleston' derives from it.

Auchenshuggle, Gaelic for 'a field of rye', was famous as the terminus for the No. 9 tram. The old village was situated behind Tollcross Central Church around the area of Easterhill Street and Corbett Street and surrounded by fields until relatively recently. Glasgow's last tramcar ran on the Auchenshuggle to Dalmuir route at the beginning of September 1962 although one of the Auchenshuggle trams enjoyed a brief revival as a pleasure ride during the Glasgow Garden Festival of 1988. These days much of the former site of Fullarton House and gardens has been developed into Auchenshuggle Wood, one of the first community nature parks. Known in the district as 'the Coosie', the eight acre site was created with the help of local volunteers who planted trees and wild flower seeds and built fences and paths with the aim of attracting wildlife to a natural habitat.